CW00432685

6202
Forfar Academy

Mealtimes

Evening Meals
Around the World

Gill Munton

WAYLAND

Mealtimes

Breakfast Around the World
Lunch Around the World
Evening Meals Around the World

Editor: Ruth Raudsepp
Designer: Joyce Chester

First published in 1998 by Wayland Publishers Limited,
61 Western Road, Hove, East Sussex, BN3 1JD, England.

Find Wayland on the internet at http://www.wayland.co.uk

British Library Cataloguing in Publication Data
Munton, Gill
Evening Meals Around the World. – (Mealtimes)
1. Dinners and dining – Juvenile literature
I. Title
394.1'5

ISBN 0 7502 1977 7

Typeset by Joyce Chester
Printed in Italy by G. Canale & C.S.p.A., Turin

Picture acknowledgements

The publishers would like to thank the following for allowing their pictures to be reproduced in this book:

Andes Press Agency/Carlos Reyes-Manzo 21; Axiom/Jim Holmes 9 (bottom); Anthony Blake Photo Library/Brian Limage 26 (bottom); Chapel Studies/Zul Mukhida 5 (top), 10, 12, 23; Bruce Coleman/Jens Rydell 8; David Cumming 28 (bottom); Sue Cunningham/SCP *title page,* 11, 24; James Davis Travel Photography/James Davis 5 (bottom), 29 (bottom); Eye Ubiquitous/Darren Maybury *contents page*, David Cumming 4 (top), Bennet Dean 6, David Cumming 14, 15, Darren Maybury 28 (top); Robert Harding/A. R. Lampshire 26 (main photo); Impact/Alain Evrard 4 (bottom right), 13, Mark Henley 16, Daniel White 17, Robert Eames 25, Alan Keohane 29 (top); Panos Pictures/CN Durrell McKenna 19; Still Pictures/Sonja Iskov *cover* (bottom); The Stockmarket/Mark Daffey *cover* (top); Tony Stone Images/Gary John Norman 9 (top); Travel Ink/Simon Reddy 18; Trip/A Tjagny-Rjadno 20; Wayland/Paul Kenward 4 (bottom left), Chris Fairclough 7, Paul Kenward 22 (both), 27.

Contents

Map of the world

The potato can be cooked in many different ways. These Russian potato cakes make a very tasty supper.

In hot countries, people often cook and eat their evening meal in the open air. Sweet potatoes and sweetcorn are both grown in Kenya.

Rice is an important part of the evening meal in Vietnam. Even very young children eat it with chopsticks.

Canadians eat a lot of meat and fish. It's good fun to cook burgers and steaks on a barbecue.

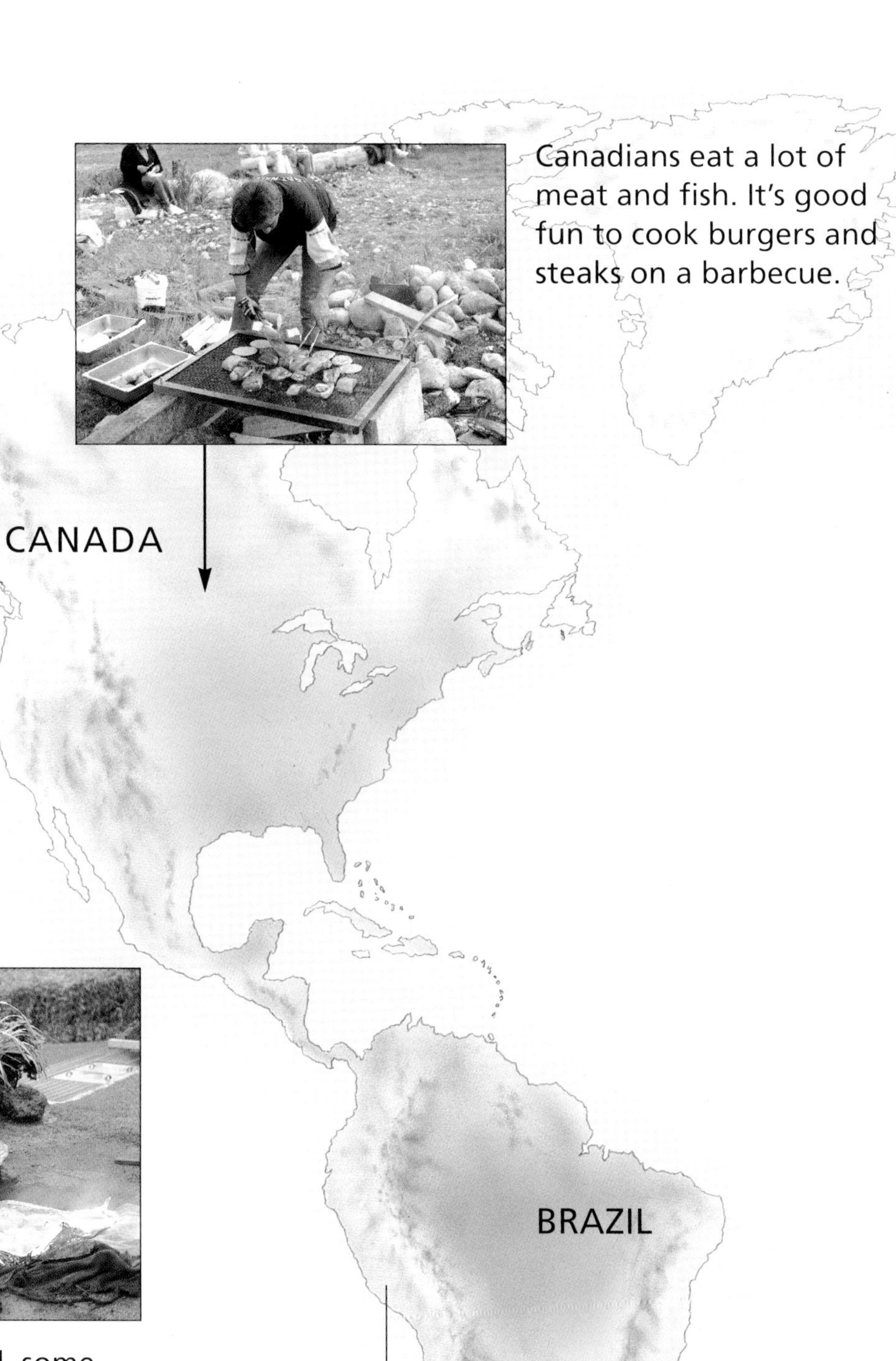

In New Zealand, some of the Maori people still cook their supper in traditional underground ovens like this one.

All the countries marked on this map are covered in this book.

Introduction

What do you like to eat for your evening meal? Perhaps you have a snack when you come home from school, or perhaps you eat supper with your family.

In this book you can find out about evening meals in lots of different countries.

Rice is nice

Rice is the most important food in many Asian countries.

The rice **seedlings** are planted under water in fields called paddies. When the seedlings are about one metre high, the water is drained away and the seedlings are harvested.

The seedlings are **threshed** so that the grains of rice fall out. These women are threshing rice in Bali, Indonesia. ►

The grains of rice are then dried in the sun. These Bangladeshi women are spreading out grains of rice with big wooden rakes. ▼

Jayani and her brother Janaka are eating rice for their supper.

They live in Sri Lanka. Their mother has served the rice with curry made from bananas. The children sit on the floor to eat, picking up the rice with their fingers.

João and his family are having supper in a restaurant.

They live on the coast in Brazil. They are sharing a bowl of rice and a big bowl of João's favourite dish, seafood.

Food for friends

Billy lives in Canada.

He is cooking supper on a barbecue for his friends. They can choose a salmon steak or a buffalo burger.

This little girl is called Lan. She lives in Vietnam.

Lan's mother has brought her to the café for a treat. While she chats with her friend, Lan eats her supper. In Vietnam most people eat with **chopsticks**.

Yuri lives in Russia. He and his Granny are having supper together.

Yuri's mother and father work in the evenings, so Granny does the cooking. Tonight she has made soup with potato cakes.

Juanita is eating dinner with her friends.

This is a tasty Spanish meal, **gazpacho** soup with **paella** and Spanish omelette.

Late suppers

Fan has a food stall in a Chinese market.

He is making **noodles**. When they are long and thin enough, Fan will fry them in hot oil and sell them as a take-away snack.

Rajiv has made a giant curry.

He has a food stall in Calcutta, India. He hopes that the people passing by will smell the curry and stop to buy some.

Salim is cooking hot, spicy sausages on his food stall.

After visiting the cinema, people crowd round his stall in Marrakesh, Morocco, to taste the delicious food.

Matthew lives in Canada. He and his friends are cooking their own late-night snack.

They are on a camping holiday. Tonight they are toasting **marshmallows** over an open fire on the beach.

Party time

Katya and her family are eating their Christmas dinner.

Katya's father is opening a bottle of champagne for them to drink with this special meal. Katya lives in Moscow, the capital city of Russia. In Russia, Christians celebrate Christmas on 7 January.

This pig is being roasted for a New Year feast.

Rajesh and Rakesh are looking forward to tasting it. They live with their families in a small village in Nepal.

Fatuma and her friends live in Kenya.

They are wearing their best clothes because they are celebrating the Muslim festival of **Eid**. Later on this evening they will eat a special meal of curry and rice.

Ali's father has a puri stall in Delhi, India.

Muslims celebrate Eid for a week. Everyone enjoys delicious food like this after their long **fast**. Food is often sold on the streets.

Hot potatoes

Patricia has cooked a large dish of potatoes for supper.

Patricia and her husband live in Peru, where potatoes were first eaten two thousand years ago.

Steve and his brothers are harvesting potatoes.

They live on a farm in Lincolnshire, Britain. Potatoes grow under the ground. This machine digs them up and separates them from the rest of the plant.

These people are watching an exciting firework display.

In Britain, Guy Fawkes Night is celebrated on 5 November with fireworks and bonfires. Some people bake jacket potatoes in the hot ashes of the fire. They eat them with steaming soup to keep out the cold.

Joseph has baked sweet potatoes over his fire.

Sweet potatoes grow in hot countries such as Kenya where Joseph lives. He has cooked some tasty sweetcorn as well.

Pots and pans

Somsri is cooking food in a wok.

She has fried some insects, and now she is straining off the oil. Insects like these are a popular food in Thailand.

Yasmin and her cousin are eating their food from banana-leaf plates.

Banana leaves are often used as plates in India. The best thing is that they don't have to be washed up after the meal. Yasmin's big sister was married today, and this is the wedding feast.

Here are two kinds of oven.

In Morocco, Mohammed is baking bread over hot coals on the ground.

Rangi has cooked some chickens in his oven in the ground.

It is a traditional oven called a **hangi**, used by the **Maori** people in New Zealand. The meat is put in a foil container and covered with wet sacking to steam.

Glossary

chopsticks Thin sticks made of ivory or wood. They are used instead of knives and forks in China, Japan and other countries in the Far East.

fast A time when people don't eat certain foods, or don't eat at all, for religious reasons.

gazpacho A Spanish vegetable soup that is eaten cold.

hangi An underground oven in which a wood fire is set under a layer of stones.

Maori The people who lived in New Zealand before the European settlers arrived.

marshmallows Sweets that are made from the roots of the marshmallow plant.

noodles Very thin strings of flour and water paste, which are boiled or fried.

paella A Spanish meal made from chicken, rice, seafood and vegetables.

puri A flat Indian bread that is made into round shapes and deep-fried.

seedlings Young plants.

threshed Beaten to remove the grains.

wok A big frying pan with a small round base, used in Eastern cooking.

Books to read

African Food and Drink by Martin Gibrill (Wayland, 1989)

Rice by Jillian Powell (Wayland, 1996)

A Taste of India by Roz Denny (Wayland, 1994)

A Taste of Spain by Bob Goodwin and Candi Perez (Wayland, 1994)

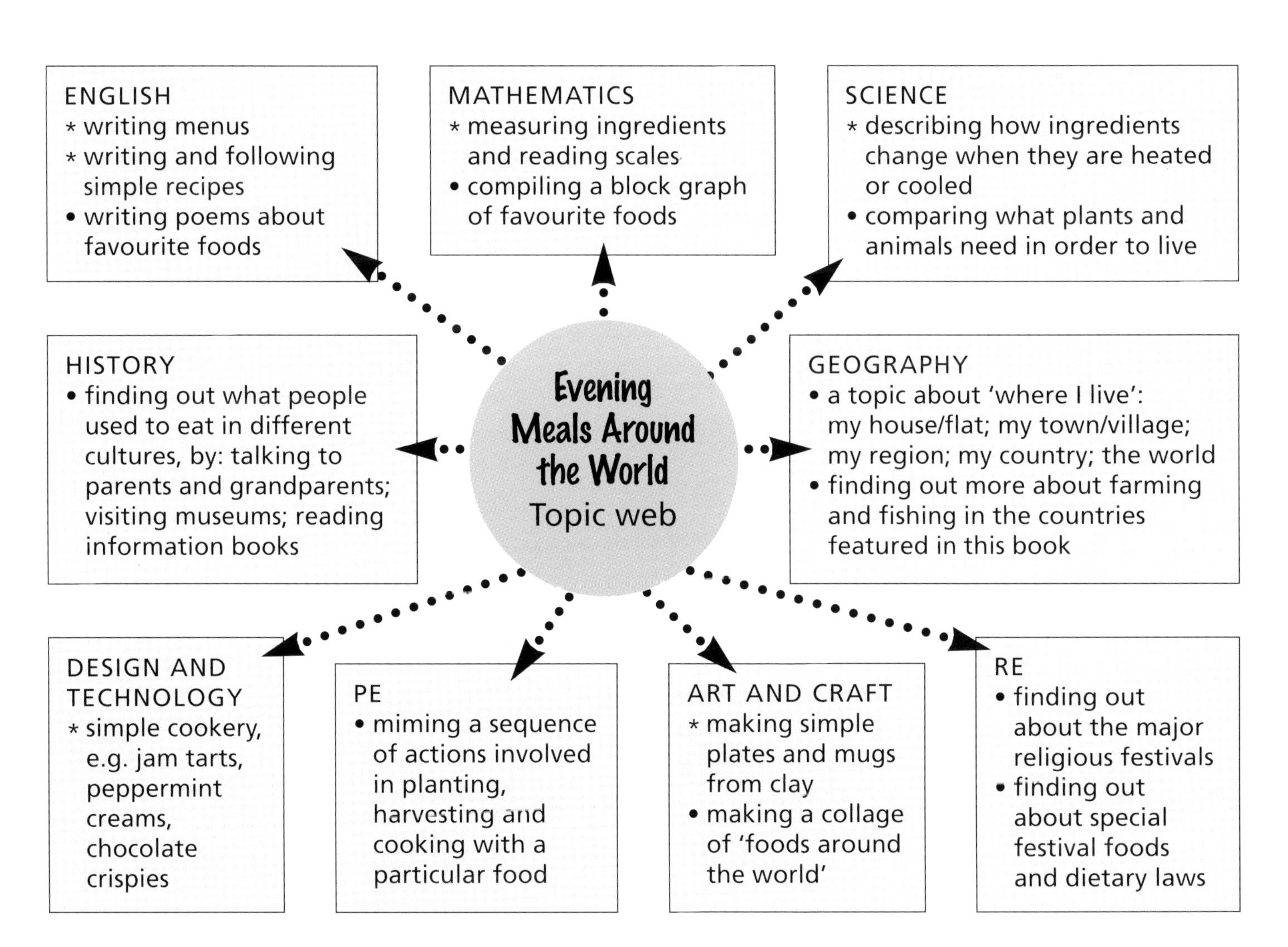

* These could be linked to form a practical cookery project.

Index